Eric Mackay

A Lover's Litanies

Eric Mackay

A Lover's Litanies

ISBN/EAN: 9783337176495

Printed in Europe, USA, Canada, Australia, Japan

Cover: Foto ©ninafisch / pixelio.de

More available books at **www.hansebooks.com**

A LOVER'S LITANIES.

A Lover's Litanies

BY

Eric Mackay

*Author of "Love Letters of a Violinist," and
"Gladys the Singer."*

1888.
LONDON:
Field & Tuer, The Leadenhall Press, E.C.
Simpkin, Marshall & Co.; Hamilton, Adams & Co.

New York: Scribner & Welford, 743 & 745, Broadway.

THE LEADENHALL PRESS,
LONDON, E.C.
T 4,258.

Ave Maria!

Contents.

	PAGE
First Litany—Virgo Dulcis	11
Second Litany—Vox Amoris	25
Third Litany—Ad Te Clamavi	39
Fourth Litany—Gratia Plena	53
Fifth Litany—Salve Regina	67
Sixth Litany—Benedicta Tu	81
Seventh Litany—Stella Matutina	95
Eighth Litany—Domina Exaudi	109
Ninth Litany—Lilium inter Spinas	123
Tenth Litany—Gloria in Excelsis	137

First Litany.

VIRGO DULCIS.

First Litany.

Virgo Dulcis.

i.

O THOU refulgent essence of all grace!
    O thou that with the witchery of thy face
Hast made of me thy servant unto death,
I pray thee pause, ere, musical of breath,
And rapt of utterance, thou condemn indeed
My venturous wooing, and the wanton speed
    With which I greet thee, dear and tender soul!
From out the fullness of my passion-creed.

ii.

I AM so truly thine that nevermore
  Shall man be found, this side the Stygian shore,
So meek as I, so patient under blame,
And yet, withal, so minded to proclaim
His life-long ardour. For my theme is just :
A heart enslaved, a smile, a broken trust,
  A soft mirage, a glimpse of fairyland,
And then the wreck thereof in tears and dust.

iii.

THOU wast not made for murder, yet a glance
  May murderous prove ; and beauty may entrance,
More than a syren's or a serpent's eye.
And there are moments when a smother'd sigh
May hint at comfort and a murmur'd " No "
Give signs of " Yes," and Misery's overflow
  Make tears more precious than we care to tell,
Though, one by one, our hopes we must forego.

iv.

I SHOULD have shunn'd thee as a man may shun
   His evil hour. I should have curst the sun
That made the day so bright and earth so fair
When first we met, delirium through the air
Burning like fire! I should have curst the moon
And all the stars that, dream-like, in a swoon
   Shut out the day,—the lov'd, the lovely day
That came too late and left us all too soon.

v.

I LOOK'D at thee, and lo! from face to feet,
   I saw my tyrant, and I felt the beat
Of my quick pulse. I knew thee for a queen
And bow'd submissive; and the smile serene
Of thy sweet face reveal'd the soul of thee.
For I was wounded as a man may be
   Whom Eros tricks with words he will not prove;
And all my peace of mind went out from me.

vi.

OH, why didst cheer me with the thought of bliss,
    And wouldst not pay me back my luckless kiss?
I sought thy side. I gave thee of my store
One wild salute. A flame was at the core
Of that first kiss; and on my mouth I feel
The glow thereof, the pressure and the seal,
  As if thy nature, when the deed was done,
Had leapt to mine in lightning-like appeal.

vii.

IF debts were paid in full I might require
    More than my kiss. I might, in time, aspire
To some new bond, or re-enact the first.
For once, thou know'st, the love for which I thirst,
The love for which I hunger'd in thy sight,
Was not withheld. I deem'd thee, day and night,
  Mine own true mate, and sent thee token flowers
To figure forth the hopes I'd fain indite.

viii.

Is this not so? Canst thou defend, in truth,
  The sunlike smile with which, in flush of youth,
Thou didst accept my greeting,—though so late,—
My love-lorn homage when the voice of Fate
Fell from thy lips, and made me twice a man
Because half thine, in that betrothal-plan
  Whereof I spake, not knowing how 'twould be
When May had marr'd the prospects it began?

ix.

Can'st thou deny that, early in the spring,
  When daisies droop'd, and birds were fain to sing,
We met, and talk'd, and walk'd, and were content
In sunlit paths? An hour and more we spent
In Keats's Grove. We linger'd near the stem
Of that lone tree on which was seen the gem
  Of his bright name, there carven by himself;
And then I stoop'd and kiss'd thy garment's hem.

X.

I GAVE thee all my life. I gave thee there,
    In that wild hour, the great Creator's share
Of mine existence ; and I turn'd to thee
As men to idols, madly on my knee ;
And then uplifted by those arms of thine,
I sat beside thee, warm'd with other wine
    Than vintage balm ; and, mindful of thy blush,
I guess'd a thought which words will not define.

xi.

I TOLD thee stories of the days of joy
    When earth was young, and love without alloy
Made all things glad and all the thoughts of things.
And like a man who wonders when he sings,
And knows not whence the power that in him lies,
I made a madrigal of all my sighs
    And bade thee heed them ; and I join'd therewith
The texts of these my follies that I prize.

xii.

I SPOKE of men, long dead, who wooed in vain
    And yet were happy,—men whose tender pain
Was fraught with fervor, as the night with stars.
And then I spoke of heroes' battle-scars
And lordly souls who rode from land to land
To win the love-touch of a lady's hand ;
    And on the strings of thy low-murmuring lute
I struck the chords that all men understand.

xiii.

I SANG to thee. I praised thee with my praise,
    E'en as a bird, conceal'd in sylvan ways,
May laud the rose, and wish, from hour to hour,
That he had petals like the empress-flower,
And there could grow, unwing'd, and be a bud,
With all his warblings ta'en at singing-flood
    And turned to vagaries of the wildest scent
To undermine the meekness in her blood.

viv.

Ah, those were days! That April should have been
  My last on earth, and, ere the frondage green
Had changed to gold, I should have join'd the ranks
Of dull dead men who lived for little thanks
And made the most thereof, though penance-bound.
I should have known that in the daily round
  Of mine existence, there are griefs to spare,
But joys, alas! too few on any ground.

xv.

And here I stand to-day with bended head,
  My task undone, my garden overspread
With baneful weeds. Am I the lord thereof?
Or mine own slave, without the power to doff
My misery's badge? Am I so weak withal,
That I must loiter, though the bugle's call
  Shrills o'er the moor, the far-off weltering moor,
Where foemen meet to vanquish or to fall?

xvi.

Am I so blurr'd in soul, so out of health,
   That I must turn to thee, as if by stealth,
And fear thy censure, fear thy quick rebuff,
And thou so gentle in a world so rough
That God's high priest, the morn-apparell'd sun
Ne'er saw thy like! Am I indeed undone
   Of life and love and all? and must I weep
For joys that quit me, and for sands that run?

xvii.

To-morrow's dawn will break; but Yesterday,
   Where is its light? And where the breezes' play
That sway'd the flowers? A bird will sing again,
But not so well. The wind upon the plain,
The wintry wind, will toss the groaning trees;
But I, what comfort shall I have of these,
   To know that they, unlov'd, have lost the Spring,
As I thy favour and my power to please?

xviii.

I SHOULD have learnt a lesson from the songs
  Of woodland birds discoursing on the wrongs
Of madcap moths and bachelor butterflies.
I should have caught the cadence of the sighs
Of unwed flowers, and learnt the way to woo,
Which all things know but I, beneath the blue
  Of Heaven's great dome ; for, undesired of thee,
I have but jarr'd the notes that seem'd so true.

xix.

I SHOULD have told thee all I meant to tell,
  And how, at Lammas-tide, a wedding-bell
Rang through my sleep, mine own as well as thine ;
And how I led thee, smiling, to a shrine
And there endow'd thee with the name I bear ;
And how I woke to find the morning-air
  Flooded with light. I should have told thee this
And not conceal'd the theme of my long prayer.

XX.

But I was timid. Oh, my love was such
    I scarce could name it ! Trembling over-much
With too much ardour, I was moved at length
To mere mad utterance. In a blameful strength
I seiz'd thy hand, to scare thee, as of old
Dryads were scared ; and calm and icy-cold
    Thine answer came : " I pray thee, vex me not !"
And all that day 'twas winter on the wold.

Second Litany.

VOX AMORIS.

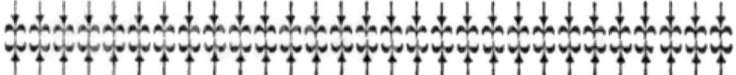

Second Litany.
Vox Amoris.*

i.

VOUCHSAFE, my Lady! by the passion-flower,
　　And by the glamour of a moonlit hour,
And by the cries and sighs of all the birds
That sing o'nights, to heed again the words
Of my poor pleading! For I swear to thee
My love is deeper than the bounding sea,
　　And more conclusive than a wedding-bell,
And freer-voiced than winds upon the lea.

---

* This Litany was introduced in the Author's "Gladys the Singer," published by Messrs. Reeves & Turner, London, 1887.

ii.

In all the world, from east unto the west,
    There is no vantage-ground, and little rest,
And no content for me from dawn to dark,
From set of sun to song-time of the lark,
And yet, withal, there is no man alive
Who for a goodly cause to make it thrive,
    Would do such deeds as I would gird me to
Could I but win the pearl for which I dive.

iii.

It is thy love which, downward in the deep
    Of far-off visions, I behold in sleep,—
It is thy pearl of love which in the night
Doth tempt my soul to hopes I dare not write,—
It is this gem for which, had I a crown,
I'd barter peace and pomp, and ermined gown ;
    It is thy troth, thou paragon of maids !
For which I'd sell the joys of all renown.

iv.

I would attack a panther in its den
    To do thee service as thy man of men,
Or front the Fates, or, like a ghoul, confer
With staring ghosts outside a sepulchre.
I would forego a limb to give thee life,
Or yield my soul itself in any strife,
   In any coil of doubt, in any spot
When Death and Danger meet as man and wife.

v.

It is my solace, all my nights and days,
    To pray for thee and dote on thee alwàys,
And evermore to count myself a king
Because I earn'd thy favour in the spring.
Oh, smile on me and call me to thy side,
And I will kneel to thee, as to a bride,
   And yet adore thee as a saint in Heaven
By God ordained, by good men glorified!

vi.

I WILL acquaint thee with mine inmost thought
 And teach thee all I know, though unbesought,
And make thee prouder of a poet's dream
Than wealthy men are proud of what they seem.
If thou have trust therein, if thou require
Service of me, or song, or penance dire,
 I will obey thee as thy belted knight,
Or die to satisfy thy heart's desire.

vii.

AH! thou hast that in store which none can give,
 None but thyself, and I am fain to live
To watch the outcome of so fair a gift,—
To see the bright good morrow loom and lift,
And know that thou,—unpeer'd beneath the moon,—
Untamed of men,—untutor'd to the tune
 Of lip with lip,—wilt cease thy coy disdain
And learn the languors of the loves of June.

viii.

All that I am, and all I hope to be,
    Is thine till death ; and though I die for thee
Each day I live ; and though I throb and thrill
At thoughts that seem to burn me, and to chill,
In my dark hours, I revel in the same ;
Yet I am free of hope, as thou of blame,
    And all around me, wakeful and in sleep,
I weave a blessing for thy soul to claim.

ix.

Oh, by thy radiant hair and by the glow
    Of thy full eyes,—and by thy breast of snow,—
And by the buds thereof that have the flush
Of infant roses when they strive to blush,—
And by thy voice, melodious as a bell
That rings for prayer in God's high citadel,—
    By all these things, and more than I can urge,
I charge thee, Sweet ! to let me out of hell !

x.

IS it not Hell to live so far away
    And not to touch thee,—not by night or day
To be partaker of one smile of thine,
Or one commingling of thy breath and mine,
Or one encounter of thine amorous mouth?
I dwell apart from thee, as north from south,
    As east from western ways I dwell apart,
And taste the tears that quench not any drouth.

xi.

WHY wouldst thou take the memory of a wrong
    To be thy shadow all the summer long,
A thing to chide thee at the dead of night,
A thing to wake thee with the morning light
For self-upbraiding, while the wanton bird
Invests the welkin? Ah, by joy deferr'd,
    By peace withheld from me,—do thou relent
And dower my life to-day with one love-word!

xii.

Wouldst thou, Cassandra-wise, oppress my soul
  With more unrest, and Hebè-like, the bowl
Of festal comfort for a moment raise
To my poor lips, and then avert thy gaze?
Wouldst make me mad beyond the daily curse
Of thy displeasure, and in wrath disperse
  That halcyon draught, that nectar of the mind,
Which is the theme I yearn to in my verse?

xiii.

Oh, by thy pity when so slight a thing
  As some small bird is wounded in the wing,
Avert thy scorn, and grant me, from afar,
At least the right to love thee as a star,—
The right to turn to thee, the right to bow
To thy pure name and evermore, as now,
  To own thy thraldom and to sing thereon,
In proud allegiance to mine earliest vow.

xiv.

It were abuse of power to frown again
    When, all day long, I gloat upon the pain
Of pent-up hope, my joy and my distress,—
While the remembrance of a mute caress
Given to a rose,—a rose I pluck'd for thee,—
Seems as the withering of the world to me,
    Because I am unlov'd of thee to-day
And undesired as sea-weeds in the sea.

xv.

I'll not believe that eyes so bright as thine
    Were meant for malice in the summer-shine,
Or that a glance thereof, though changed to fire,
Could injure one whose spirit, like a lyre,
Has throbb'd to music of remember'd joys,—
The pride thereof, and all the tender poise
    Of trust with trust,—the symphonies of grief
Made all mine own,—and Faith which never cloys.

xvi.

How can it be that one so fair as thou
    Should wear contention on a whiter brow
Than May-day Dian's in her hunting gear?
I'll not believe that eyes so holy-clear
And mouth so constant to its morning prayer
Could mock the mischief of a man's despair
    And all the misery of a moment's hope
Seen far away, as mists are seen in air.

xvii.

How can a woman's heart be made of stone
    And she not know it? Mine is overthrown.
I have no heart to-day, no perfect one,
Only a thing that sighs at set of sun
And beats its cage, as if the thrall thereof
Were freedom's prison or the tomb of love;
    As if, God help me! there were shame in truth
And no salvation left in realms above.

xviii.

I once could laugh, I once was deem'd a man
    Fit for the frenzies of the dead god Pan,
And now, by Heaven! the birds that sing so well
Move me to tears; and all the leafy dell,
And all the sun-down glories of the West,
And all the moorland which the moon has blest,
    Make me a dreamer, aye! a coward, too,
In all the weird expanse of mine unrest.

xix.

It is my curse to see thee and to learn
    That I must shun thee, though I blaze and burn
With all this longing, all this fierce delight
Fear-fraught and famish'd for a suitor's right;
A right conceded for a moment's space
And then withdrawn as, amorous face to face,
    I dared to clasp thee and to urge a troth
Too sovereign-sweet for one of Adam's race.

XX.

I am a doom-entangled mirthless soul,
    Without the power to rid me of the dole
Which, day by day, and nightly evermore
Corrodes my peace! Oh, smile, as once before,
At each wild thought and each discarded plea,
And let thy sentence, let thy suffrance be
    That I be reckon'd till the day I die
The sad-eyed Singer of thy fame and thee!

Third Litany.

AD TE CLAMAVI.

Third Litany.

Ad Te Clamavi.

i.

AGAIN, O Love! again I make lament,
    And, Arab-like, I pitch my summer-tent
Outside the gateways of the Lord of Song.
I weep and wait, contented all day long
To be the proud possessor of a grief.
It comforts me. It gives me more relief
    Than pleasures give ; and, spirit-like in air,
It re-invokes the peace that was so brief.

ii.

IT speaks of thee. It keeps me from the lake
   Which else might tempt me ; and for thy sweet sake
I shun all evil. I am calmer now
Than when I wooed thee, calmer than the vow
Which made me thine, and yet so fond withal
I start and tremble at the wind's footfall.
   Is it the wind ? Or is it mine own past
Come back to life to lure me to its thrall ?

iii.

I LONG to rise and seek thee where thou art
   And draw thee amorous to my wakeful heart
That beats for thee alone, in vague unrest.
I long to front thee when thou'rt lily-dress'd
In white attire,—e'en like the flowers of old
That Jesus praised ; and. though the thought be bold,
   I'm fain to kiss thee, Sweetheart ! through thy hair
And hide my face awhile in all that gold.

iv.

I will not say what more might then be done,
　And how, by moonlight or beneath the sun,
We might be happy.　In a reckless mood
I've talk'd of this ; and dreams and many a brood
Of tongue-tied fancies have my soul beset.
I will not hint at fealty or the fret
　Of lips untrue, or anger thee therein,
Or call to mind one word thou wouldst forget.

v.

I should withhold my raptures were I wise,
　I should not vex thee with my many sighs,
Or claim one tear from thee, though 'tis my due.
I should be silent.　I should cease to sue !
Sorrow should teach me what I fail'd to learn
In days gone by ; and cross'd at every turn
　By some new doubt, new-born of my desires,
I should suppress the pangs with which I burn.

THIRD LITANY.

vi.

I AM an outcast from the land of love
    And thou the Queen thereof, as white as dove
New-sped from Heaven, and fine and fair to see
As coy Queen Mab when, out upon the lea,
She met her master and was lov'd of him.
Thou art allied to long-hair'd cherubim,
    And I a something undesired of these,
With woesome lips and eyes for ever dim.

vii.

I WAS ordain'd thy minstrel, but alas!
    I dare not greet the when I see thee pass;
I scarce, indeed, may hope at any time,
To work my will, or triumph in a rhyme
To do thee honour; no, nor make amends
For unsought fervor, in the tangled ends
    Of my despair. How sad, how dark to me
All things have grown since thou and I were friends!

viii.

It is the fault of thy despotic glance,
  It is the memory of a day's romance
When, true to thee, though taunted for my truth,
I dared to solemnise the joys of youth
In one wild chant. It is thy fault, I say !
Thy piteous fault that, on the verge of May,
  I lost the right to live, as heretofore,
Untouched by doubt from day to brightening day.

ix.

O Summer's Pride ! I loved thee from the first,
  And, like a martyr, I was blest and curst,
And saved and slain, and crown'd and made anew,
A grief-glad man, with yearnings not a few,
But no just hope to win so fair a troth.
I should have known how one may weep for both
  When lovers part, poor souls ! beneath the moon,
And how Remembrance may outlive an oath.

x.

The nymphs, I think, were like thee in the glade
    Of that Greek valley where the wine was made
For feasts of Bacchus ; for I dream at night
Of those creations, kind and calm and bright ;
And in my thought, unhallow'd though it be,
The sun-born Muses turn their gaze on me,
    And seem to know me as a friend of theirs,
Though all unfit to serve them on my knee.

xi.

They lived and sang. They died as visions die,
    Supreme, eternal, offshoots of the sky,
Made and re-made, undraped and draped afresh,
To glad the earth like phantoms made of flesh,
And yet as mistlike as delusions are !
They stood beside Achilles in his car ;
    They knew the gods and all their joysome deeds,
And all the chants that sprang from star to star.

xii.

The myths of Greece, the maidens of the grove,
    The dear dead fancies of the days of Jove,
Why were they bann'd? Oh, why in Reason's name,
Were they abolished? They were good to claim,
And good to dream of, and to crown with bays,
Far-seen of men, far-shining in the haze
    Of withering doubts. They were the world's elect,
As thou art mine, to bow to and to praise.

xiii.

Night after night I see thee, in my dreams,
    As fair as Daphne, with the morning beams
Of thy bright locks about thee like a cloak,—
Fair as the young Aurora when she woke
At Phæthon's call, athwart the mountain-heights.
I see thee radiant in the summer nights,
    And, bosom-pack'd with frenzies unrepress'd,
I thrill to thee in Slumber's soft delights.

xiv.

I see thee pout. I see thee in disdain
  Look out, reluctant, through the falling rain
Of thy long hair. I feel thee close at hand.
I note thy breathing as I loose the band
That binds thy waist, and then to waking life
I backward start! Despair is Sorrow's wife;
  And I am Sorrow, and Despair's mine own,
To lure me on to madness or to strife.

xv.

My sex offends thee, or the thought of this;
  For I did fright thee when I fleck'd a kiss
With too much heat. I should have bow'd to thee,
And left unsaid the word, deception-free,
Which, like a flash, illumed the love within,
My wilfulness was much to blame therein;
  But thou wilt shrive me, Sweet! of mine offence
If passion-pangs be deem'd so dark a sin.

xvi.

Oh, give me back my soul that with the same
    I may achieve a deed of poet-fame,
Or die belauded on the battle-field !
There's much to seek. My hand is strong to wield
Weapon or pen. If thou consent thereto
Deeds may be done. If not, thine eyes are blue
    And Heaven is there,—a twofold tender shrine
Whose wrath I fear, whose judgment still I rue !

xvii.

I am but half myself. The life in me
    Is nigh crush'd out ; and, though I seem to see
Glory, and grace, and joy, as in the past,
They are but shadows on the cozening blast,
And dreams of devils and distorted things,
And snakes coiled up that look like wedding rings,
    And faded flowers that once were fit for wreaths
In bygone summers and in perish'd springs.

xviii.

THERE is a curse in every garden place,
    And when, at night, the lily's holy face
Looks up to God, it seems to chide me there.
The very sun with all his golden hair
Is ill at ease, and birth and death of day
Bring no relief; and darkly on my way
    My memory comes,—the ghost of my Delight,—
To fret and fume at woes it cannot slay.

xix.

OH, bid me smile again, as in the time
    When all the breezes seem'd to make a chime,
And all the birds on all the woodland slopes
Had trills for me, and seem'd to guess the hopes
That warm'd my heart. O thou whom I adore!
How proud were I,—though wounded bitter-sore
    By shafts of doubt,—if, in default of love
I could but win thy friendship as of yore.

XX.

THEN were I blest indeed, and crown'd of fate
    As kings are crowned, as bards in their estate
Are rapture-fraught, re-risen above the dust.
Then were I torture-proof, and on the crust
Of one kind word, though as a pittance thrown,
I'd live for weeks! My tears I would disown
    And pray, contented with my discontent,
As hermits pray when storms are overblown.

Fourth Litany.

GRATIA PLENA.

Fourth Litany.

Gratia Plena.

i.

O^H, smile on me, thou syren of my soul !
    That I may curb my thoughts to some control
And not offend thee, as in truth I do,
Morning, and noon and night, when I pursue
My vagrant fancies, unallow'd of thee,
But fraught with such consolement unto me
    As may be felt in homeward-sailing ships
When wind and wave contend upon the sea.

ii.

Dower me with patience and imbue me still
    With some reminder, when the night is chill,
Of thy dear presence, as, in winter-time,
The maiden moon, that tenderly doth climb
The lofty heavens, hath yet a beam to spare
For doleful wretches in their dungeon-lair;
    E'en thus endow me in my chamber dim
With some reminder of thy face so fair!

iii.

Quit thou thy body while thou sleepest well
    And visit mine at midnight, by the spell
That knows not shame. For in the House of Sleep
All things are pure; and in the silence deep
I'll wait for thee, and thou, contrition-wise,
Wilt seek my couch and this that on it lies,
    This frame of mine that lives for thee alone
As palmers live for peace that never dies.

iv.

It were a goodly thing to spare a foe
    And kill his hate. And I would e'en do so !
For I would kill the coyness of thy face.
I would enfold thee in my spurn'd embrace
And kiss the kiss that gladdens as with wine.
Yea, I would wrestle with those arms of thine,
    And, like a victor, I would vanquish thee,
And, tyrant-like, I'd teach thee to be mine.

v.

For, what is peace that we should cling thereto
    If war be wisest ? If the death we woo
Be fraught with fervor there's delight in death !
There is persuasion in the tempest's breath
Not known in calm ; and raptures round us flow
When, like an arrow through the bended bow
    Of two fond lips, the quivering dart of love
Brings down the kiss which saints shall not bestow.

vi.

The soldier dies for country and for kin;
    He dies for fame that is so sweet to win;
And, part for duty, part for battle-doom,
He wends his way to where the myrtles bloom;
He gains a grave, perchance a recompense
Beyond his seeking, and a restful sense
    Of soul-completion, far from any strife,
And far from memory of his land's defence.

vii.

Be this my meed,—to die for love of thee,
    As when the sun goes down upon the sea
And finds no mate in all the realms of earth.
I, too, have look'd on Nature in its worth
And found no resting-place in all the spheres,
And no relief beyond my sonnet-tears,—
    The soul-fed shudderings of my lonely harp
That knows the gamut now of all my fears.

viii.

I wear thy colours till the day I die:
   A glove, a ribbon, and a rose thereby,
All join'd in one. I revel in these things;
For, once an angel, unarray'd in wings,
Came to my side, and beam'd on me, and said:
"I love thee, friend!" and then, with lifted head,
   Gave me a rose on which the dew had fallen;
And, like the flower, she blush'd a virgin-red.

ix.

I found the glove down yonder in the dale.
   I knew 'twas thine; its color, creamy-pale,
Fill'd me with joy. "A prize!" I cried aloud,
And snatch'd it up, as zealous then, and proud,
As one who wins a knighthood in his youth;
And I was moved thereat, in very sooth,
   And kiss'd it oft, and call'd on kindly Heaven
To be the sponsor of mine amorous truth.

x.

I EARN'D the ribbon as we earn a smile
   For service done. I help'd thee at the stile ;
And so 'twas mine, my trophy, as of right.
Oh, never yet was ribbon half so bright !
It seem'd of sky-descent,—a strip of morn
Thrown on the sod,—a something summer-worn
   To be my guerdon ; and, enriched therewith,
I follow'd thee, thy suitor, through the corn.

xi.

I TROD on air. I seem'd to hear the sound
   Of fifes and trumpets and the quick rebound
Of bells unseen,—the storming of a tower
By imps audacious, and the sovereign power
   Of some arch-fairy, thine acquaintance sure
In days gone by ; for, all the land was pure,
   As if new-blest,—the land and all the sea
And all the welkin where the stars endure.

xii.

WE journey'd on through fields that were a-glow
   With cowslip buds and daisies white as snow ;
And, hand in hand, we stood beside a shrine
At which a bard whom lovers deem divine,
Laid down his life ; and, as we gazed at this,
There seem'd to issue from the wood's abyss
   A sound of trills, as if, in its wild way,
A nightingale were pondering on a kiss.

xiii.

A LANE was reached that led I know not where,
   Unless to Heaven,—for Heaven was surely there
And thou so near it ! And within a nook
A-down whose covertness a noisy brook
Did talk of peace, I learnt of thee my fate ;
The word of pity that was kin to hate,—
   The voice of reason that was reason's foe
Because it spurn'd the love that was so great !

xiv.

But I must pause. I must, from day to day,
    Keep back my tears, and seek a surer way
Than Memory's track. I must, with lifted eyes,
Re-shape my life, and heed the battle-cries
Of prompt ambition, and be braced at call
To do such deeds as haply may befall,
    If, freed of thee, and charter'd to myself,
I may undo the bonds that now enthrall.

xv.

Shall I do this? I shall; and thou shalt see
    Signs of rebellion. I will turn to thee
And claim obedience. I will make it plain
How many a link may go to form a chain,
And each a circlet, each a ring to wear.
I will extract the sting from my despair
    And toy therewith, as with a charmèd snake,
That, Lamia-like, uprears itself in air.

xvi.

OR is my boast a vain, an empty one,
    And shall I rue it ere the day is done?
Will hope revive betimes? Or must I stand
For evermore outside the fairyland
Of thy good will? Alas! my place is here,
To muse and moan and sigh and shed my tear,
  My paltry tear for one who loves me not,
And would not mourn for me on my death-bier.

xvii.

OH, get thee hence, thou harbinger of light!
    That, like a dream, dost come to me at night
To haunt my sleep, and rob me of content,
So true-untrue, so deaf to my lament,
I must forego the pride I felt therein.
Aye, get thee hence! And I will crush the sin,
  If sin it be, that prompts me, night and day,
To seek in thee the bliss I cannot win.

xviii.

Or, if thou needs must haunt me after dark,
    Come when I wake. The oriole and the lark
Are friends of thine ; and oft, I know, the thrush
Has trill'd of thee at morn and even-blush.
And flowers have made confessions unto me
At which I marvel ; for they rail at thee
    And call thee heartless in thy seemlihood,
Though queen-elect of all the flowers that be.

xix.

Nay, heed me not! I rave ; I am possess'd
    By utmost longing. I am sore oppress'd
By thoughts of woe ; and in my heart I feel
A something keener than the touch of steel,
As if, to-day, a danger unforeseen
Had track'd thy path,— as if my prayers had been
    Misjudged in Heaven, or drown'd in demon-shouts
Beyond the boundaries of the coasts terrene.

XX.

But this is clear ; this much at least is true :
   I am thine own ! I doat upon the blue
Of thy kind eyes, well knowing that in these
Are proofs of God ; and down upon my knees
I fall subservient, as a man in shame
May own a fault ; albeit, as with a flame,
   I burn all day, abash'd and unforgiven,
And all unfit to touch the hand I claim !

Fifth Litany.

SALVE REGINA.

Fifth Litany.

Salve Regina.

i.

Glory to thee, my Queen! whom far away
    My thoughts aspire to,—as the birds of May
Aspire o' mornings,—as in lonely nooks
The gurgling murmurs of neglected brooks
Aspire to moonlight,—aye! as earth aspires
When through the East, alert with wild desires,
    The rapturous sun surveys the welkin's height,
And flecks the world with witcheries of his fires.

ii.

OH, I should curb my grief. I should entone
  No plaint to thee ; no loss should I bemoan !
I should be patient, I, though full of care,
And not attempt, by bias of a prayer,
To sway thy spirit, or to urge anew
A claim contested. For my days are few ;
  My days, I think, are few upon the earth
Since I must shun the joys I would pursue.

iii.

I AM not worthy of the Heaven I name
  When I name thee ; and yet to win the same
Is still my dream. I strive as best I can
To live uprightly on the vaunted plan
Of old-world sages. But I strive not well ;
And thoughts conflicting which I cannot quell
  Make me despondent ; and I quake thereat,
As at the shuddering of a doomsday bell.

IV.

To die for thee were more than my desert;
   To live for thee to keep thee out of hurt
And, like a slave, to wait upon thy will
Were more than fame. And lo! I nourish still
A sense of calm to feel that thou, at least,
Art sorrow-free and honor'd at the feast
   Which Nature spreads for all contented minds;
And that for thee its splendours have increased.

V.

I stand alone. I stand beneath the trees,
   I guess their thoughts; I hear them to the breeze
Say tender nothings; and I dream the while
Of thy white arms, and thy remember'd smile,
When, in a spot like this, a year a-gone,
I saw thee stoop to pluck from off the lawn
   A wounded bird that peer'd into thy face
As if it took thee for the nymph of dawn!

vi.

OH, can it be, as friends of thine affirm
    That thou'rt a fairy,—that, from term to term,
Month after month, belov'd of all good things,
Thou'rt seen in forests and in meadow rings
Girt for the dance ? or like an Oread queen
Array'd for council ? For the woods convene
    Their dryad forces when the nights are clear,
And nymphs and fawns carouse upon the green.

vii.

THE crescent moon, the Argosy of heaven,
    Veers for the west across the Pleïads seven,
And, out beyond the ridge of Charles's Wain,
It seems to come to mooring on the main
Of that deep sky, as if awaiting there
An angel-guest with sunlight in her hair,
    A seraph's cousin, or the foster-child
Of some centurion of the upper air.

viii.

Is it thy soul? Has Cynthia call'd for thee
  In her white boat, to take thee o'er the sea
Where suns and stars and constellations bright
Are isles of glory,—where a seraph's right
Surpasses mine, and makes me seem indeed
A base intruder, with a coward's creed
  And not an angel's, though a Christian born
And pledged alwàys to serve thee at thy need?

ix.

Thou'rt sleeping now; and in thy snowy rest,—
  In that seclusion which is like a nest
For blameless human maids beheld of those
Who come from God,—thou hast in thy repose
No thought of me,—no thought of pairing-time.
For thou'rt the sworn opponent of the rhyme
  That lovers make in kissing; and anon
My very love will vex thee like a crime.

x.

But day and night, and winter-tide and spring,
    Change at thy voice; and when I hear thee sing
I know 'tis May; and when I see thy face
I know 'tis Summer. Thou'rt the youngest Grace,
And all the Muses praise thee evermore.
And there are birds who name thee as they soar;
   And some of these,—the best and brightest ones,—
Have guess'd the pangs that pierce me to the core.

xi.

Thou art the month of May with all its nights
    And all its days transfigured in the lights
Of love-lit smiles and glances multiform;
And, like a lark that sings above a storm,
Thy voice o'er-rides the tumult of my mind.
Oh, give me back the peace I strove to find
   In my last prayer, and I'll believe that Hope
Will dry anon the tears that make it blind.

xii.

There's none like thee, not one in all the world;
    No face so fair, no smile so sweet-impearl'd,
And no such music on the hills and plains
As thy young voice whereof the thrill remains
For hours and hours,—belike to keep alive
The sense of beauty that the flowers may thrive.
  Or is't thy wish that birds should fly to thee
Before the days of April's quest arrive?

xiii.

Thou'rt noble-natured; and there's none to stand
    So meek as thou, or with so dear a hand
To ward off wrong. For Psyche of the Greeks
Is dead and gone; and Eros with his freaks
Has bow'd to thee, and turn'd aside, for shame,
His useless shaft, not daring to proclaim
  His amorous laws, and thou so maiden-coy
Beneath the halo of thy spotless name!

xiv.

But dreams are idle, and I must forget
    All that they tend to. I must cease to fret,
Moth as I am, for stars beyond the reach
Of mine up-soaring; and in milder speech
I must invoke thy blessing on the road
That lies before me,—far from thine abode,
    And far from all persuasion that again
Thou wilt accept the terms of my love-code.

xv.

O Sweet! forgive me that from day to day
    I dream such dreams, and teach me how to sway
My fluttering self, that, in forsaken hours,
I may be valiant, and eschew the powers
Of death and doubt! I need the certitude
Of thine esteem that I may check the feud
    Of mine own thoughts that rend and anger me
Because denied the boon for which I sued.

XVI.

TEACH me to wait with patience for a word,
  And be the sight of thee no more deferr'd
Than one up-rising of the vesper star
That waits on Dian when, supreme, afar,
She eyes the sunset. And of this be sure,
As I'm a man and thou a maid demure,
 Thou shalt be ta'en aside and wonder'd at,
Before the gloaming leaves the land obscure.

XVII.

THOU shalt be bow'd to as we bow to saints
  In window'd shrines; and, far from all attaints
Of ribald passion, thou, as seemeth good,
Wilt smile serenely in thy virginhood.
Nor shall I know, of mine own poor accord,
Which thing in all the world is best to hoard,
 Or which is worst of all the things that slay:
A woman's beauty or a soldier's sword.

xviii.

I GRIEVE in sleep. I pine away at night.
  I wake, uncared for, in the morning light ;
And, hour by hour, I marvel that for me
The wandering wind should make its minstrelsy
So sweet and calm. I marvel that the sun,
So round and red, with all his hair undone,
   Should smile at me and yet begrudge me still
The sight of thee that art my worshipp'd one !

xix.

I COUNT my moments as a cloister'd man
   May count his beads ; and through the weary span
Of each long day I peer into my heart
For hints of comfort ; and I find, in part,
A self-committal, and a glimpse withal
Of some new menace in the rise and fall
   Of days and nights that are the test of Time
Though Fate would make a mockery of them all.

XX.

There's a disaster worse than loss of gold,
    Worse than remorse, and worse a thousand-fold,
Than pangs of hunger. 'Tis the thirst of love,
The rage and rapture of the ravening dove
We name Desire. Ah, pardon! I offend;
My fervor blinds me to the withering end
    Of all good council, and, accurst thereby,
I vaunt anew the faults I cannot mend.

Sixth Litany.

BENEDICTA TU.

Sixth Litany.

Benedicta Tu.

---

i.

I TELL thee Sweet! there lives not on the earth
   A love like mine in all the height and girth
And all the vast completion of the sphere.
I should be proud, to-day, to shed a tear
If I could weep. But tears are most denied
When most besought; and joys are sanctified
   By joys' undoing in this world of ours
From dusk to dawn and dawn to eventide.

ii.

WERT thou a marble maid and I endow'd
    With power to move thee from thy seeming shroud
Of frozen splendour,—all thy whiteness mine
And all the glamour, all the tender shine
Of thy glad eyes,—ah God ! if this were so,
And I the loosener, in the summer-glow,
    Of thy long tresses ! I were licensed then
To gaze, unchidden, on thy limbs of snow.

iii.

I WOULD prepare for thee a holy niche
    In some new temple, and with draperies rich,
And flowers and lamps and incense of the best,
I would with something of mine own unrest
Imbue thy blood and prompt thee to be just.
I would endow thee with a fairer trust
    Than mere contentment, and a dearer joy
Than mere revulsion from the sins of dust.

iv.

A BAND of boys, with psaltery and with lyre,
　　And Cyprian girls, the slaves of thy desire,
Would chant and pray and raise so wild a storm
Of golden notes around thy sculptured form
That saints would hear the chorus up in Heaven,
And intermingle with their holy steven
　　The sighs of earth, and long for other cares
Than those ordain'd them by the Lord's Eleven.

v.

I WOULD approach thee with a master's tread
　　And claim thy hand and have the service read
By youthful priests resplendent every one ;
And in thy frame the blood of thee would run
As warm and sound as wine of Syracuse.
And all that day the birds would bear the news
　　In far directions, and the meadow-flowers
Would dream thereof, love-laden, in the dews.

vi.

THEN, by magnetic force,—the greatest known
 This side the tomb,—I would athwart the stone
Of thy white body, in a trice of time,
Call forth thy soul, and woo thee to the chime
Of tinkling bells, and make thee half afraid,
And half aggrieved, to find thyself array'd
 In such enthralment, and in such attire,
In sight of one whose will should not be stay'd. ·

vii.

And, like Pygmalion, I would claim anon
 A bride's submission; and my talk thereon
Would not perplex thee; for the sense of life
Would warm thy heart, and urge thee to the strife
Of lip with lip, and kiss with pulsing kiss,
Which gives the clue to all we know of bliss,
 And all we know of heights we long to climb
Beyond the boundaries of the grave's abyss.

viii.

THE dear old deeds chivalrous once again
    Would find fulfilment ; and the curse of Cain
Which fell on woman, as on men it fell,
Would fly from us, as at a sorcerer's spell,
And leave us wiser than the sophists are
Who love not folly. Night should not debar,
  Nor day dissuade us, from those ecstacies
That have Anacreon's fame for guiding-star.

ix.

AYE! thou wouldst kneel and seek in me apace
    A transient shelter for thine amorous face
Which then I'd screen ; and thou to me wouldst turn
With awe-struck eyes, and cling to me and yearn,
With sighs full tender and a touch of fear.
And, like a bird which knows that spring is near,
  And, after spring, the summer of sweet days,
Thou wouldst attune thy love-notes in mine ear.

x.

Or, fraught with feelings near akin to hate,
    Thou wouldst denounce me ; and, like one elate,
Thou wouldst entwine me in thine arms so white,
As soldier-nymphs, with rapt and raging sight,
Made war with spearsmen in the vales of song,
The vales of Sparta where, for right or wrong,
    The gods were potent, and, for beauty's sake,
Upheld the tourneys of the fair and strong.

xi.

I would not seem too wilful in the heat
    Of our encounter, or with sighs repeat
Too fierce a vow. I would throughout confess
Thy murderous mirth, thy conquering loveliness,
And then subdue thee ! Tears would not avail
Nor prayer, nor praise ; and, flush'd the while or pale,
    Thou shouldst be mine, my hostage in the night,
Without the option of a moment's bail.

xii.

Thou shouldst be mine ! My hopes, from first to last,
  Would win their way ; and, lithe and love-aghast,
And all unnerv'd, thou wouldst, as in a dream
Entreat my pardon ! I would callous seem
To thine out-yearning. I would cast on thee
A questioning look, and then, upon my knee,
I would surrender to that face of thine
Which is the great world's wonder unto me.

xiii.

O Heaven ! could this be done, and I fulfil
  One half my wish, and curb thee to my will,
I were a prompter and a prouder man
Than earth has known since light-foot lovers ran
For Atalanta, lov'd of men and boys.
I were a kaiser then, a king of joys,
  And fit to play with high-begotten pomps
As children play with pebbles or with toys.

xiv.

O GOLDEN Hair! O Gladness of an Hour
Made flesh and blood ! O beauteous Human Flower
Too sweet to pluck, and yet, though seeming-cold,
Ordain'd to love ! I pray thee, as of old,
Be kind to me. I saw thee yesternight,
And for an instant I was urged to plight
　My troth again ; for in thy face I saw
What seem'd a smile evoked for my delight.

xv.

RE-GRANT thy favour ! Take me by the hand
　And lead me back again to thine own land,
The nook supreme, the sanctum in the glen
Where pixies walk,—unknown to peevish men
And shrew-like women whom no faith uplifts !
Show me the place where Nature keeps the gifts
　She most approves, and where the song-birds dwell,
And I'll forego the land of little thrifts.

xvi.

The moon is mother and the sun is sire
    Of those young planets which, with infant fire,
Have late been found in regions too remote
For quicklier search ; and these, in time, will dote
And whirl and wanton in the realms of space.
For there are comets in the nightly chase
  Who see strange things untalk'd of by the bards ;
And earth herself has found a trysting-place.

xvii.

And so 'tis clear that sun and moon and stars
    Are link'd by love ! The marriage-feast of Mars
Was fixt long since. 'Tis Venus whom he weds.
'Tis she alone for whom he gaily treads
His path of splendour ; and of Saturn's ring
He knows the symbol, and will have, in spring,
  A night-betrothal, near the Southern Cross ;
And all the stars will pause thereat and sing.

xviii.

WHAT wonder, then, what wonder if to-day
    I, too, assert my right, in roundelay,
To talk of rings and posies and the vows
That wait on marriage? 'Tis the wild carouse
Of soul with soul athwart the sense of touch.
'Tis this uplifts us when, with fever-clutch,
    The world would claim us; and our hopes revive
In spite of fears that daunt us over-much.

xix.

LIPS may be coy; but eyes are quick, at times,
    To note the throbbings that are hot as crimes,
And fond as flutterings of the wings of doves.
For he is blind indeed who, when he loves,
Doubts all he sees :—the flickering of a smile,
The Parthian glance, the nod that, for a while,
    Outbids Elysium, and is half a jest,
And half a truth, to tempt us and beguile.

XX.

THINE eyes have told me things I dare not speak ;
    And I will trust the track they bid me seek,
Yea, though it lead me to the gates of death !
The wind is labouring :—it is out of breath ;
Belike for scampering up the hill so fast
To say all's well with thee ; and, down the blast,
    I seem to hear the sounds of serenades
That swell from out the song-fields of the past.

Seventh Litany.

STELLA MATUTINA.

Seventh Litany.

Stella Matutina.

i.

ARISE, fair Phœbus ! and with looks serene
    Survey the world which late the orbèd Queen
Did pave with pearl to please enamour'd swains.
Arise ! Arise ! The Dark is bound in chains,
And thou'rt immortal, and thy throne is here
To sway the seasons, and to make it clear
    How much we need thee, O thou silent god !
That art the crown'd controller of the year.

ii.

And while the breezes re-construct for thee
The shimmering clouds; and while, from lea to lea,
The great earth reddens with a maid's delight,
Behold ! I bring to thee, as yesternight,
My subject song. Do thou protect apace
My peerless one, my Peri with the face
  That is a marvel to the minds of men,
And like a flower for humbleness of grace.

iii.

The earth which loves thee, or I much have err'd,
  The glad, green earth which waits, as for a word,
The sound of thee, up-shuddering through the morn,
The restive earth is pleased when Day is born,
And soon will take each separate silent beam
As proof of sex,—exulting in the dream
  Of joys to come, and quicken'd and convuls'd,
Year after year, by love's triumphant theme.

iv.

A THOUSAND times the flowers in all the fields
    Will bow to thee ; and with their little shields
The daisy-folk will muster on the plain.
A thousand songs the birds will sing again,
As sweet to hear as quiverings of a lute ;
And she I love will sing, for thy repute,
    Full many a song. She sings when she but speaks ;
And when she's near the birds should all be mute.

v.

O MY Belovèd ! from thy curtain'd bed
    Arise, rejoice, uplift thy golden head,
And be an instant, while I muse on this,
As nude as statues, and as good to kiss
As dear St. Agnes when she met her death,
Unclad and pure and patient of her breath,
    And with the grace of God for wedding-gown,
As many an ancient story witnesseth.

vi.

THE bath, the plunge, the combing of the hair,
    All this I view,—a sight beyond compare
Since Daphne died in all the varied charms
Of her chaste body,—rounded regal arms,
And shape supreme, too fair for human gaze,
But not too fair to win the mirror's praise
    That throbs to see thee in thy déshabille
And loves thee well through all the nights and days.

vii.

I SEE thee thus in fancy, as in books
    A man may see the naïads of the brooks,—
As one entranced by potions aptly given
May see the angels where they walk in Heaven,
And may not greet them in their high estate.
For who shall guess the riddle wrought of Fate
    Till he be dead? And who that lives a span
Shall thwart the Future where it lies in wait?

viii.

And now to-day a word I dare not write
    Starts to my lips, as when a baffled knight
Witholds a song which fain he would repeat ;
For lo ! the sense thereof is passing sweet.
And, like a cup that's full, my heart is fill'd
With new desires and quiverings new-distill'd
    From old delights ; and all my pulses throb
As at the touch of dreams divinely-will'd.

ix.

Who talks of comfort when he sees thee not
    And feels no fragrance of the happy lot
Which violets feel, when call'd upon to lie
On thy white breast ? And who with amorous eye
Looks at the dear tomb of the shuddering flowers,
The two-fold tomb where daintily for hours
    They droop and muse,—who looks, I say, at these
And will not own the witchery of thy powers ?

x.

WHO speaks of glory and the force of love,
    And thou not near, my maiden-minded dove!
With all the coyness, all the beauty-sheen,
Of thy rapt face? A fearless virgin-queen,—
A queen of peace art thou,—and on thy head
The golden light of all thy hair is shed
    Most nimbus-like and most suggestive, too,
Of youthful saints enshrined and garlanded.

xi.

THOU'RT Nature's own ; and when a word of thine
    Rings on the air, and when the Voice Divine
We call the lark upfloats amid the blue,
I know not which is which, for both are true,
Both meant for Heaven, though foster'd here below.
And when the silences around me flow,
    I think of lilies and the face of thee
Which hath compell'd my manhood's overthrow.

xii.

O BLUE-EYED Rapture with the radiant locks !
    O thou for whom, athwart the fever-shocks
Of life and death and misery and much sin,
I'd sell salvation ! There's a prize to win
And thou'rt its voucher ; there's a wonder-prize,
Unknown till now beneath the vaulted skies,
    And thou'rt its symbol ; thou'rt its essence fair,
Its full completion form'd adoring-wise !

xiii.

YES, I will tell thee how I love thee best,
    And all my thoughts of thee shall be confess'd
And none withheld, not e'en the witless one
Which late I harbor'd when the mounting sun
Burst from a cloud,—the moon a mile away,
As if in hiding from the lord of day,—
    As if, at times, the moon were like thyself,
And fear'd the semblance of a master's sway.

XIV.

I LOVE thee dearly when thine eyes are dim
    With unshed tears; for then they seem to swim
In liquid blessedness, and unto me
There comes the memory of a god's decree
Which said of old :—" Be all men evermore,
All men and maids whose hearts are passion-sore,
    Acclaim'd in Heaven !" and all day long I muse
On hope's divine and deathless prophet-lore.

XV.

I LOVE thee when the soft endearing flush
    Invades thy face, and dimples in the blush
Bespeak attention,—as a rose's pout
Absorbs the stillness when the sun is out,
And all the air retains the glow thereof.
In all the world there is not light enough
    Nor sheen enough, all day, nor any warmth,
Till thou be near me, arm'd with some rebuff !

xvi.

And how I love thee when thy startled eyes
    Look out at me, enrapt in that surprise
Which marks an epoch in the life I lead,—
As if they guess'd the scope of Eros' creed
And all the mirth and malice of his wiles.
For it is wondrous when my Lady smiles,
   And all the ground is holy where she treads,
And all the air is thrill'd for many miles!

xvii.

In every mood of thine thou art my joy,
    And, day by day, to shield thee from annoy,
I'd do the deeds that slaves were bound unto
With stabs for payment,—shuddering through and through
With their much labour; and I'd deem it grand
To die for thee if, after touch of hand,
   I might but kiss thee as a lover doth;
For I should then be king of all the land.

xviii.

But Father Time, old Time with Janus-face
  Looks o'er the sphere, and sees no fitting place
For thine acceptance ; for the thrones of earth
Are much too mean, and in thy maiden worth
Thou'rt crown'd enough, and throned in very sooth
More than the queens who lord it in their youth
  O'er men's convictions ; and He names thy name
As one belov'd of Nature and of Truth.

xix.

He sees the nights, he sees the veering days,
  The sweet spring season with its hymn of praise,
The summer, frondage-proud, the autumn pale,
The winter worn with withering of the gale,—
All this he sees ; and now, to-day, in June,
He, too, recalls that rapturous afternoon
  When all the fields and flowers were like a dream,
And all the winds the offshoot of a tune.

XX.

So I will cease to clamour for the past,
    And seek suspension of my doubts at last,
In some new way till Fate becomes my friend.
I will re-gain the right to re-defend
The love I bear to thee, for good or ill.
For though, 'tis said, our griefs have power to kill,
    Mine let me live, in mine unworthiness,
That, spurn'd of thee, my lips may praise thee still!

Eighth Litany.

DOMINICA EXAUDI.

Eighth Litany.

Domina Exaudi.

i.

IT seems a year, and more, since last we met,
    Since roseate spring repaid, in part, its debt
To thy bright eyes, and o'er the lowlands fair
Made daffodils so like thy golden hair
That I, poor wretch, have kiss'd them on my knees!
Forget-Me-Nots peep out beneath the trees
    So like thine eyes that I have question'd them,
And thought thee near, though viewless on the breeze.

ii.

It seems a year ; and yet, when all is told,
 'Tis but a week since I was re-enroll'd
Among thy friends. How fairy-like the scene !
How gay with lamps ! How fraught with tender sheen
Of life and languor ! I was thine alone :—
Alert for thee,—intent to catch the tone
 Of thy sweet voice,—and proud to be alive
To call to heart a peace for ever flown.

iii.

Had I not vext thee, as a monk in prayer
 May vex a saint by musing, unaware,
On evil things ? A saint is hard to move,
And quick to chide, and slow,—as I can prove,—
To do what's just ; and yet, in thy despite,
We met again, we too, at dead of night ;
 And I was hopeful in my love of thee,
And thou superb, and matchless, in the light.

iv.

I FELT distraught from gazing over-much
    At thy great beauty; and I fear'd to touch
The dainty hand which Envy's self hath praised.
I fear'd to greet thee ; and my soul was dazed
And self-convicted in its new design ;
For I was mad to hope to call thee mine,
    Aye ! mad as he who claims a Virgin's love
Because his lips have praised her at a shrine.

v.

I SAW thee there in all the proud array
    Of thy young charms,—as if a summer's day
Had leapt to life and made itself a queen,—
As if the sylphs, remembering what had been,
Had mission'd thee, from out the world's romance,
To stir my pulse, and thrill me with a glance :
    And once again, allow'd, though undesired,
I did become thy partner in the dance.

vi.

I bow'd to thee. I drew thee to my side,
   As one may seize a wrestler in his pride
To try conclusions,—and I felt the rush
Of my heart's blood suffuse me in a blush
That told its tale. But what my tongue would tell
Was spent in sighs, as o'er my spirit fell
   The silvery cadence of thy lips' assent;
And every look o'er-ruled me like a spell.

vii.

O DEVIL's joy of dancing, when a tune
   Speeds us to Heaven, and night is at the noon
Of all its frolic, all its wild desire!
O thrall of rapt illusions when we tire
Of coy reserve, and all the moments pass
As pass the visions in a magic glass,
   And every step is shod with ecstacy,
And every smile is fleck'd with some Alas!

DOMINICA EXAUDI.

viii.

Was it a moment or a merry span
   Of years uncounted when convulsion ran
Right through the veins of me, to make me blest,
And yet accurst, in that revolving quest
Known as a waltz,—if waltz indeed it were
And not a fluttering dream of gauze and vair
   And languorous eyes? I scarce can muse thereon
Without a pang too sweet for me to bear!

ix.

By right of music, for a fleeting term,
   Mine arms enwound thee and I held thee firm
There on my breast,—so near, yet so remote,
So close about me that I seem'd to float
In sunlit rapture,—touch'd I know not how
By some suggestion of a deeper vow
   Than men are 'ware of when, on Glory's track,
They kneel to angels with uplifted brow.

x.

And lo! abash'd, I do recall to mind
　　All that is past :—the yearning undefined,—
The baulk'd confession that was like a sob—
The sound of singing and the gurgling throb
Of lute and viol,—meant for many things
But most for misery ; and a something clings
　　Close to my heart that is not wantonness,
Though, wanton-like, it warms me while it stings.

xi.

The night returns,—that night of all the nights!
　　And I am dower'd anew with such delights
As memory feeds on ; for I walk'd with thee
In moonlit gardens, and there flew to me
A flower-like moth, a pinion'd daffodil,
From Nature's hand ; and, out beyond the hill,
　　There rose a star I joy'd to look upon
Because it seem'd the star of thy good will.

xii.

WE sat beneath the trees, as well thou know'st,
   Within an arbour which a summer's boast
Had made ambrosial; and we loiter'd there
Some little space, the while upon the air
Uprose the fragrance of uncounted flowers.
Ah me! how weird a tryste was that of ours!
   And how the moon look'd down, so lurid-warm,
Athwart the stillness of the frondage-towers!

xiii.

I SEEM'D to feel thy breath upon my cheek;
   I vainly searched for words I long'd to speak,
But could not utter lest the sound thereof
Should scare away the elves that wait on love.
And when I spoke to thee 'twas of the spot
Where we were seated,—things that matter'd not,—
   Uncared for things,—the weather,—the new laws!
And, sudden-loud, the wind assail'd the grot.

xiv.

A LITTLE bird was warbling overhead
    As if to twit me with the word unsaid
Which he, more daring, when the sun was high,
Trill'd to his mate! He knew the tender "why"
Of many a pleading, and he knew, meseems,
The very key-note to the lyric dreams
    Of all true poets when, by love impell'd,
They search the secrets of the woods and streams.

xv.

'TIS sure that summer, when she rear'd the bower
    And arched the roof and gave it all the dower
Of all its leaves, and all the crannies small
Where wrens look through,—'tis sure that, after all,
Summer was kind, and meant to make for me
A shriving-place,—a lighthouse on the sea
    Of all that verdure,—that, beneath the stars,
I might receive one quickening glance from thee.

xvi.

OH! had I dared to whisper in thine ear
   My heart-full wish, undaunted by the fear
Of some rebuke :—a flush of thy fair face,
A lifted hand to tell me that the place
Was fairy-fenced, and guarded as by flame,—
Oh! had I dared to court the word of blame
   That's good for me, no doubt! at every turn,
My life to-day were chasten'd by the same.

xvii.

BUT I was conscious of a sudden ban
   Hurl'd from the zenith. I was like the man
Who scaled Olympus, with intent to bring
New fire therefrom, and dared not face the King
Of thought and thunder. I was full prepared
For thy displeasure,—for the past was bared
   To mine on-looking; and, with faltering tongue,
I left my languorous meanings undeclared.

xviii.

O LOST Occasion ! what a thing art thou :—
A three-fold key,—the when, the where, the how,—
The past, the present and the future tense,—
All thrown aside. For what ? A witless sense
Of some compunction ! When the hour is bold
Reason is shy, and rapture, seeming-cold,
Makes mute surrender of its dearest chance,
And all for fear of doubts that might be told.

xix.

BUT could we meet, oh ! could we meet again
On some such night, unseen upon the plain,
I'd rob thee, Lady ! of a tard'y smile.
I would do this ; and, for a breathing-while,
I would assert a sinner's right to pray,
A sinner's right to choose, as best he may,
His patron-saint ; and I would kneel to thee,
And call thee mine, and dote on thee for aye !

XX.

And then in summer, when the hours are mad,
    And all the flow'rets in the fields are glad,
And all the breezes, like demented things
Outspeed the birds with sunlight on their wings,
In summer, aye! in summer's gracious time,
I might perchance be pardon'd for the crime
    Of my much love, and win thy benison
Ere yet the year has reached its golden prime!

✜✜✜✜✜✜✜✜✜✜✜✜✜✜✜✜✜✜

Ninth Litany.

LILIUM INTER SPINAS.

✜✜✜✜✜✜✜✜✜✜✜✜✜✜✜✜✜✜

Ninth Litany.

Lilium inter Spinas.

i.

DEAREST and best of maidens, whom the Fates
    Have dower'd with beauty, whom the glory-gates
Have shown so splendid in my waking sight,
Is't well, thou syren! thus to haunt the night
And grant no mercy, none from week to week
All through the year? Is't well my soul to seek
    And shun my body? Is't throughout ordain'd
That thou shouldst spurn a love so tender-meek?

ii.

IT is my joy to serve thee, 'tis my pride
  To own my follies, though anew denied
The chance of wisdom, and for this, who knows?
I shall be counted, ere the season's close,
A time-perverter. Yes! I shall be shamed,
And frown'd upon, and day by day proclaim'd
  A foe to virtue, though, in seeking thee
I seek the goal that Virtue's self hath named.

iii.

O LILY mine! O Lily tipp'd with gold
  And welkin-eyed for angels to behold
When down on earth! Is't well to stand apart
And gaze at me and gently break my heart
Without one word? Is't well to seem alwày
So grieved to see me, when, at fall of day,
  Thou dost accept the reverence of mine eyes,
But not the homage that my lips would pay?

iv.

Oh, give me back again, at midnight hour,
    As in the circuit of that starlit bower,
The right to talk with thee, and be thy friend,—
The right, in some wild way, to make an end
Of my submission, or to re-bestow
My troth on thee,—despite the overthrow
    Of all my dreams, that were my constant care,
Though less to thee than flakes of alien snow.

v.

I will unveil my meanings one by one,
    And tell thee why the bird that loves the sun
Loves not the moon, though conscious of her fame.
For he's the soul of truth, in his acclaim,
And knows not treason! And of like intent
Are all my yearnings, too, when I lament.
    And, though I say it, there's no troubadour
Has lov'd as I, since Cupid's bow was bent.

vi.

I HAVE been wed in sleep, and thou hast been
    Mine own true bride,—the swooning summer-queen
Of my heart-throbs. I have been wed in jest!
I have been taken wildly to thy breast,
And then repell'd, and made to feel the ire
Of eager eyes that have the strange desire
    To rack my soul, a-tremble in the dark,
But not the will to aid me to aspire.

vii.

I SHOULD have died the instant that I heard
    Thy whisper'd vow in slumber,—when a word
Made me thy master, for I did receive
Thy full surrender, and I'll not believe
That all was false ; or that my dreaming-power
Was given for nought. The Future may devour
    The facts of earth, but not its phantasies,
And not the dreams we dream from hour to hour.

viii.

OH, thou'lt confess that love from man to maid
    Is more than kingdoms,—more than light and shade
In sky-built gardens where the minstrels dwell,
And more than ransom from the bonds of Hell.
Thou wilt, I say, admit the truth of this,
And half relent that, shrinking from a kiss,
   Thou didst consign me to mine own disdain,
Athwart the raptures of a vision'd bliss.

ix.

I'LL seek no joy that is not link'd with thine,
    No touch of hope, no taste of holy wine,
And, after death, no home in any star
That is not shared by thee, supreme, afar,
As here thou'rt first and foremost of all things!
Glory is thine and gladness and the wings
   That wait on thought when, in thy spirit-sway,
Thou dost invest a realm unknown to kings.

x.

I WILL accept of thee a poison-bowl
    And drink the dregs thereof,—aye! to the soul,—
And sound thy praises with my latest breath!
I was a pilgrim bound for Nazareth,
But when I knew thee, when I touched thy hand,
I changed my purpose; and to-day I stand
    Thine amorous vassal, though denounced afresh
And warn'd away, unkiss'd, from Edenland.

xi.

O FLOWER unequall'd here from morn to morn,
    Is 't well, bethink thee, with a rose's thorn
To deck thyself, thou lily! and to seem
So irresponsive to my passion-dream?
Is 't a caprice of thine to look so proud,
And so severe, athwart the shining cloud
    Of thy long hair? And shall I never learn
How least to grieve thee when my vows are vow'd?

xii.

THE full perfection of thy face is such
    That, like a child's, it seems to know the touch
Of some glad hour that God has smiled upon.
There is a whiteness whiter than the swan,
A singing sweeter than the linnet's note.
But there is nothing whiter than thy throat,
   And nothing sweeter than thy tender voice
When, love-attuned, it skyward seems to float.

xiii.

LILY and rose in one! To find thy peer
    Exceeds belief, all through the varying year,
For chance thereof, and hope thereof, is none.
There comes no rival to the rising sun,
And none to thee!—no rival to the moon
That sets in Venice on the far lagoon,
   And none to thee, thou marvel of the months,
That art the cynosure of night and noon!

xiv.

Yes, I will hope. I will not cease to turn
   My thoughts to thee, and cry to thee, and yearn
As one in Hell may lift enamour'd eyes
To some sweet soul beyond the central skies
Whose face has slain him! For 'tis true, I swear:
I have been murder'd by thy golden hair,
   And by the brightness of those fringèd orbs
That are at once my joy and my despair.

xv.

Winter is wild; but spring will come again;
   For there's compunction in the fever-pain
That earth endures when, clamorous down the steep,
The wind out-blows the curse it cannot keep.
And so, belike, thy scorn of me may change
To something fairer than the fated range
   Of dole, and doubt, and pity, and reproof;
And then my sighs may cease to seem so strange.

xvi.

For thou and I will meet and not be foes,
    E'en as the rue may stand beside the rose
And not affront it,—as a lonely tree
May guard a shrine and not upon the lea
Be deem'd obtrusive,—as an errant knight
May serve the sovereign of his soul's delight
    And not, thereby, be deem'd of less account
Than he who keeps her daily in his sight.

xvii.

Reject me not that in the world of men,
    Among the wielders of the sword and pen
I have, as 'twere, detractors by the score,—
Reject me not for faults that I deplore
And fain would alter,—though, if I were wise,
I'd blunt the edge thereof in some disguise
    Approved of thee! For I've a kind of hope
That we'll be friends again ere summer dies.

xviii.

IF this be true I'll greet thee with such fire
　　That thou wilt throb thereat, as throbs a lyre,
And give thine answer, too, without restraint,
And neither frown at me nor fear a taint
In my much zeal, that knows not any pause
But, night and day, is constant to the laws
　　Of its own making, and is fain to prove
How leagued it is throughout to Honor's cause.

xix.

I WILL conceal from thee no thought of mine.
　　All will be clear as signing of a sign
On marriage-scrips ; and, though I tell thee so,
The seas and streams of earth shall cease to flow
Ere thou shalt find, in this world or the next,
A love so proud, a faith so firmly sex'd,
　　As this of mine. For thou'rt the polar star
To which I turn as minstrel to his text.

XX.

But woe's the hour ! My heart is wounded sore,
    And soon may cease to take, as heretofore,
Such keen delight in tears that comfort not,
But evermore do seem to leave a blot
On sorrow's teaching ! Shall I muse thereon
One season more, till hope and faith be gone ?
    Or must I look for comfort up in Heaven
And then be slain by thee as night by dawn ?

Tenth Litany.

GLORIA IN EXCELSIS.

Tenth Litany.

Gloria in Excelsis.

i.

O Love! O Lustre of the sunlit earth
    That knows thy step and revels in the worth
Of thy much beauty! Is't thy will anew,
Famed as thou art, to marvel that I sue
With such persistence, and in such unrest
Amid the frenzies of my passion-quest?
    Wilt look ungently, and without a tear,
On all the pangs I bear at thy behest?

ii.

Morning and eve I cease not, when I kneel
　　To my Redeemer for my spirit's weal
And for my body's,—as becomes a man,—
Morning and eve I cease not in the span
Of all my days, O thou Unconquer'd One!
To pray for thee, and do what may be done
　　To re-acquire the friendship I have lost,
Which is the holiest thing beneath the sun.

iii.

For what is fame that with so loud a voice
　　O'ersways the nations? What the random choice
Of sight and sound which makes the place we fill
So fraught with good, so redolent of ill?
Where is the thunderstorm of yesternight
That shook the clouds? And where the levin's blight
　　That spake of chaos and the Judgment Day?
And where the wisdom of a king's delight?

iv.

Could I be kiss'd of thee, or crown'd of men,
    I'd choose the kiss. I'd be ordainèd then
Lord of myself, and not the slave I seem
To each new doubt. Our tryste was like a dream
And yet 'twas true. For oft, by wonder-chance,
We find the path to many a bright romance,
    And many a tilt and tourney of dear love
In which the brave are vanquish'd by a glance.

v.

To lie alone with thee one little hour,
    And cling to thee as flower may cling to flower,
With no rough thought beyond the peace thereof,—
To be thy comrade, and to don and doff
The little chain that hangs about thy neck,—
To do all this, my Fair One! and to fleck
    Thine eyes with kisses, were a righteous deed,
And not a thing for Love to hold in check.

vi.

Nay, there are dimples which I long to taste,
   And there's a girdle fit for Phœbe's waist
Which I would loosen ; for I have the skill
To handle lilies ; and, by Venus' will,
I'd handle thee, and comfort thee therein.
For love's a sacrament I'd die to win,
   And not a toy nor yet a subterfuge ;
And not a pitfall for the feet of sin.

vii.

The searching suddenness of thy blue eyes,
   The flash thereof, the fire that in them lies,—
All this I yearn to,—all the soul of thee
Shown in thy looks, as though to solace me
In some disaster portion'd out as mine.
Where thou abidest, where thy limbs recline,
   Where thou'rt absorb'd in silence or in prayer,
There stands a throne, there gleams a fairy shrine.

viii.

I AM, indeed, more subject to thy sway
    Than trees are subject, in their tender way,
To earth's great king revolving round the sphere.
I am thy suffering servant all the year ;
And when I wake thy name is on my lips,
And when I sleep I feel thy finger-tips
    Press'd on mine eyes, as if thy wraith were there,
To save my soul from night's entire eclipse.

ix.

TILL I have heard from thee my doom of death
    I shall be proud to serve thee with my breath,
And with my labour, and be thine withal
As Man is God's,—content with any thrall
That's bound in thee ; content with any lot
That's link'd with thine, in some secluded spot
    Which thou hast lov'd, O Lady ! in the past,
And where remorse and wrong will find us not.

X.

To know thee fair, ah God ! how sweet is this ;
   To find thee wavering, and to grasp in bliss
Only the dream of thee, how sad the while !
And yet, by reason of a moment's smile,
How grand to hope, how gracious to forget !
Thou false to me ? Thou heedless of a debt
   Of love's incurring ? Nay, by Juno's crown,
Thy snow-white hand shall be my guerdon yet !

xi.

The spirit-love that leads us to the soul
   Athwart the body as its fairest goal,—
The love that lives in languor undefined
And yet is strong,—the love that can be kind
And yet aggressive as a soldier's blade,
Keen to the hilt, entranced and not afraid,—
   This is the love that will survive the death
Of all endowments which the years have made.

xii.

WILT frown at this? Wilt chide me? Wilt appeal,
As some are wont, when lovers, out of zeal,
O'erstep the bounds of wisdom which hath ceased
To win men's praise? The Matins of the East
Sung by the lark,—the Credo of the Cloud
Which oft he sings in confirmation proud
  Of his great love,—all this were mine excuse
If I could sing as he, so dawn-endow'd.

xiii.

FOR I'd be welcome, then, where'er thou art,
And gladden thee, and play as prompt a part
As Romeo play'd with Juliet at his breast.
Who loves not love, who hates to be caress'd,
Is Nature's bane ; and I'll denounce him, too.
For he 's a foe to all that's just and true
  In earth and Heaven ; and when he seeks a joy,
His quest shall fail,—his hand shall miss the clue.

xiv.

WE know these things. We know how dark a word
   May let in light, and how the smallest bird
May mix the morn with music till we think
The fire-lit air is wine for us to drink,—
And every drop salvation,—every sound
A Muse's whisper,—all the flower-full ground
   A fancy carpet fit for knights to tread
When on their way to Arthur's Table Round.

xv.

A PEEVISH fool is he who will not raise
   His hands in prayer, among the danger-days
That come to all ; for he, when waxen old,
Will search the past and find it callous-cold ;
And all the future, too, will freeze for him.
Nor shall he weep aright when tears bedim
   His desperate, doleful eyes that know not faith ;
And he shall hear no chants of cherubim.

xvi.

I was bewitch'd of late ! My soul had met
   Some fearful doom ; and there had dropt a threat,—
A curse belike,—from lips of Atropos.
There had been done a deed of spirit-loss
Which did o'erwhelm me as I paused thereat.
But now 'tis shunn'd ; and where a Tremor sat
   Now sits a Hope ; and where a gulf was seen
Now stands a mount as blest as Ararat.

xvii.

The rose is silent, and the lily dumb
   For Man alone. He sees them when they come
Glad from the soil ; but what they mean thereby,
And what they dream of, when they front the sky,
Eludes his learning. But the birds can tell.
Moths talk to flowers ; and breezes in the dell
   Hear more confessions than we men reveal ;
And oaks and cedars love each other well.

xviii.

IN woodland places where the grass is lit
    With lamp-like flowers, I seem to see thee flit
On azure wings, as if to bless the glade ;
For, everywhere, thy form in shine and shade
Doth come and go, conversant, as I deem,
With Nature's whims ; for thou'rt of great esteem
    In fairy haunts ; and elves and fays confess
How sweet thou art, my Love ! and how supreme.

xix.

DIANA'S self was not more virgin-proud.
    The maiden-moon, new-seated on a cloud
That seems her throne where she receives the stars,—
The moon who holds her court beyond the jars
Of land and sea,—the moon, the vestal moon,
Has kept thee cold since the transcendant noon
    Of that wild day when I thy hand did claim,
And when thy lips refusèd me their boon.

XX.

But thoughts are free ; and mine have found at last
    Their apt solution ; and, from out the past,
There seems to shine as 'twere a beacon-fire ;
And all the land is lit with large desire
Of lambent glory ; all the quivering sea
Is big with waves that wait the Morn's decree,
    As I, thy vassal, wait thy beckoning smile
Athwart the splendors of my dreams of Thee !

Amen !

THE LEADENHALL PRESS
LONDON, E.C
T 4,258.

www.ingramcontent.com/pod-product-compliance
Lightning Source LLC
Chambersburg PA
CBHW030342170426
43202CB00010B/1214